THE ALLEN
ILLUSTRATED GUIDE TO
TRAINING
AIDS

THE ALLEN
ILLUSTRATED GUIDE TO
TRAINING
AIDS

HILARY VERNON

J. A. ALLEN · LONDON

British Library Cataloguing-in-Publication Data.
A catalogue record for this book is available from the British Library

ISBN 0.85131.760.X

© Hilary Vernon, 2000
Hilary Vernon asserts her right to be identified as the author of this work
in accordance with the Copyright, Design and Patent Act 1988.

No part of this book may be reproduced, stored in a retrieval system, or
transmitted, in any form or by any means, electronic, mechanical, photocopying,
recording or otherwise, without the prior permission
of the publisher. All rights reserved.

First published in Great Britain 2000
Reprinted 2002

J.A. Allen
Clerkenwell House
Clerkenwell Green
London EC1R 0HT

J.A. Allen is an imprint of Robert Hale Limited

Design and Typesetting by Paul Saunders
Illustrations by Maggie Raynor
Colour separation by Tenon & Polert Colour Scanning Ltd.
Printed in China by Midas Printing International Co. Ltd.

I would like to dedicate this book to the memory of my father Harold Vlies for all the years of unstinting love and encouragement even though he thought horses were best viewed from the other side of a gate.

CONTENTS

ACKNOWLEDGEMENTS

I would like to thank: Quanah Holland, a friend for many years, who lent me books and faxed through numerous helpful articles; Daan Zylmans, UK representative of Bieman de Haas, for boxes of very interesting schooling equipment and English translations; Kate Cox of Blacknest Gate Training Centre for patiently spending hours in the cold with Bodie, both being guineapigs; Richard Waygood for trying out different pieces of equipment and reporting back; Maggie Raynor for her excellent illustrations and, finally, my husband Andrew for taking numerous photos for this book and for all his support

1 WHY USE TRAINING AIDS AT ALL?

MOST OF THE SCHOOLING EQUIPMENT or training aids that we see today were invented for, and should be used for, specific purposes: to relax, school, build, develop and discipline horses for all sorts of equestrian uses. If applied correctly and knowledgeably many do make a significant difference. But before you use a piece of schooling equipment or a training aid I suggest you think carefully about a few of the following points.

Have I made a fair assessment of my horse's mental state?

As suggested in my first book, *The Allen Illustrated Guide to Bits and Bitting*, in order to be able to begin to school or train a horse fairly you must be sure that he is mentally able to cope with what you are trying to achieve. If his diet is too high in protein for his temperament or his workload for instance, or if he is not allowed any freedom and only has an hour's hack around the block or half an hour cantering around in the school on the end of a lunge line in his headcollar, he may be genuinely difficult to handle and ride or drive, but this might not be improved by buying an expensive training aid. Go through your horse's lifestyle to see if you can make changes and improvements. What you perceive to be a schooling problem could be erratic behaviour caused by over-excitement.

Most of us have to work for a living and fit our horses in before and after work. After eight or nine hours at work not many of us feel like changing and mucking out and schooling our horses, particularly in the dark and in the cold! So, after all the chores are done and we are tired it's not surprising that the prospect of riding our horses for two hours or more is daunting. But your horse has possibly stood in his stable for 20 hours awaiting release.

If overfeeding and underexercising isn't enough to cope with, there is the possibility that not enough hay is being fed to satisfy his need for fibre. If you leave your horse at night at 8pm, and do not go to the yard until 7am or 8am the next morning and his night hay ration only lasted until 10pm he has had 10 hours in which to do nothing but wait anxiously for you to arrive to feed him again. If your horse is being badly behaved or will not relax sufficiently to be schooled because of any of these factors, then better management is required, not the use of a schooling device.

Is my horse physically comfortable and fit enough?

A check should always be kept on your horse's soundness; if he is a little pottery or not 100 per cent sound, using some of the powerful training aids will only make things worse, not better. Teeth need regular attention: any sharp edges are going to make it difficult for the horse to accept a bit and establish a good head carriage if his head and mouth are not comfortable. The bridle and saddle should fit comfortably and correctly. Any rugs should fit well so that they do not rub sores on the shoulders and withers, a driving horse's breast collar harness may touch parts of his shoulder that are already sore from rug rubs. A horse should be kept at a comfortable temperature; some of our winters can be very mild and rugging up a horse so that he is constantly sweating will only make him miserable and possibly cause skin eruptions that make him uncomfortable. No horse is going to respond well to new ideas and pieces of strange equipment unless he is calm and comfortable and reasonably fit and well. Most of the training aids require a horse to maintain certain physical shapes; if the horse is not very fit he will soon get tired and begin to resist because it is simply not comfortable to carry on.

Sound application of basic knowledge

As with all well-thought-out ideas everything is open to misuse through lack of knowledge and even, in some cases, to abuse. If you are struggling with a specific problem and are thinking of using a piece of schooling equipment, you really need to have a clear idea of what your problems are, what you expect to achieve, exactly which item of schooling equipment will best suit the goal you wish to reach and, most importantly, which piece of schooling equipment will suit your horse's conformation. If your horse has weak conformation this could possibly be the source of your problem. Great care must be taken to build up and improve a weakness, not cause distress by the wrong approach. You are trying to achieve a relaxed, interested and obedient horse not a tired, bored, tense one. Nothing should be rushed, there are no short cuts, allow yourself time to slowly build the horse's confidence, obedience and gradually his strength and physique.

Force and coercion

In my opinion horses should not be coerced into submission but fairly and systematically schooled so that they enjoy the work being asked of them. If what you are doing with your horse is not working, take a mental step back and reassess the situation. Are you trying to force your horse into a shape that he is not physically capable of achieving at this level of training? Are you lungeing or schooling too often and for too long using a schooling aid that is not fitted correctly thus causing resistances stemming from discomfort? If you feel that there are no changes to be made, seek help and advice, there are plenty of well-qualified people to turn to. You may have to try one or two until you find someone you really feel confident with. I am not saying that certain horses do not need very skilled and firm handling but with thought and a well-executed schooling plan, even the cheekiest and brightest can be made to conform. There are no short cuts to a well-schooled and calmly obedient horse willing to do things for his rider out of understanding and a physical wellbeing.

Powerful tools in the wrong hands

Some pieces of schooling equipment are very powerful tools indeed and some can put great strain on the horse's limbs and back. A gradual introduction is always necessary, a gentle, slow build-up of short sessions over a period of time, with correctly fitted and applied training aids, will always achieve more in the long term than forced and prolonged sessions of misunderstanding and fatigue. Remember to vary your work, continuous repetitive schooling is very boring, use what facilities you have well: flat work, pole work, gymnastic jumping, everything to produce a satisfied relaxed and happy horse.

In the following chapters I have tried to set out clearly with photographs, illustrations and simple text what each piece of schooling equipment looks like, how it should be fitted and what it is designed to do.

2 LUNGEING

LUNGEING is a form of schooling that can be used throughout a horse's active life. Control is primarily through the lunge rein reinforced by the trainer's voice and, to a lesser extent, the lunge whip. Lungeing teaches the horse to trust, understand and obey the trainer and helps to build concentration, muscle structure, rhythm, strength and patience. With a young horse in particular you hope to achieve all this without the unaccustomed and difficult-to-balance weight of the rider on the horse's back.

The main uses of lungeing are:
• the early training of a young horse;
• suppling exercises for horses in work;
• retraining of older horses;
• establishing schooling practices for horses coming back into work after a break;
• exercising horses that cannot be ridden;
• initial exercise for a horse that is overexuberant before being ridden;
• advanced schooling work;
• training riders to help with co-ordination and balance.

Voice commands
Voice commands must be simple, clear and different from each other so that the horse can easily recognise and understand each one and not get confused by two words sounding the same. You need to decide which words you will use for each command and say the same word each time. All upward transition words should be said with an upward lift to the voice, encouraging the horse to move forward and increase the pace, all downward transition words should have a downward, low tone to them and be long and drawn out to allow the horse time to execute the movement. I always

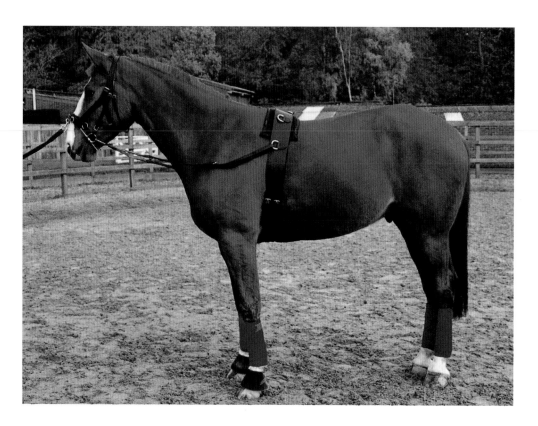

the horse correctly
prepared for lungeing

use the horse's name first in all upward transitions, once the horse knows his name it becomes easy to gain his attention. In the training of carriage horses, when driving more than one horse at a time, by using a horse's name, it is possible to single out one horse without making the others respond as well. If one horse is hanging back, for example, you call his name and, because each horse is accustomed to move forward in response to his name, he pays attention and moves up into his collar. No other horse should respond as they will know you were not speaking to them. With a voice command for all the horses you use something like 'boys, walk on' or 'everybody, walk on'.

The correct equipment

Using the correct equipment for lungeing your horse will make the task much easier; everything must be well-made and strong. It is very important to lunge correctly because so much damage can be done if the horse is allowed to just gallop around a small circle in only a cavesson or headcollar on a lunge line.

Remove excess equipment

As with all pieces of schooling equipment, any unnecessary tack should not be used. If you are not going to ride immediately after lungeing take the reins off your bridle. If you are to ride straight away make sure that the reins are firmly secured so that there is no possibility of the horse's hooves getting caught up in them or the horse receiving a nasty slap in the eye. Unsecured pieces of equipment hanging and flapping around the horse are very dangerous and distracting and with certain horses very frightening. Any such incidents caused by loose equipment can be potentially dangerous or, if you get away without serious accident, could result in the horse being reluctant to be lunged in the future.

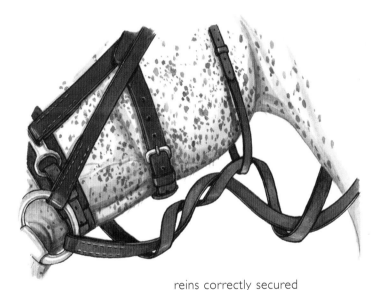

reins correctly secured

Saving time

If you are using your lunge work as a prelude to your ridden work, rather than have to go back to the yard to spend time changing from lungeing equipment to riding gear, by far the best way is to lunge by placing the lungeing roller over the saddle. It is far easier to fit pieces of schooling equipment to the easy-to-reach and numerous D rings provided on a lungeing roller than to have them slip to different levels under the saddle flap of your saddle. Then, when you are ready to ride you only need to remove the outer lungeing equipment and the horse is ready to work under saddle.

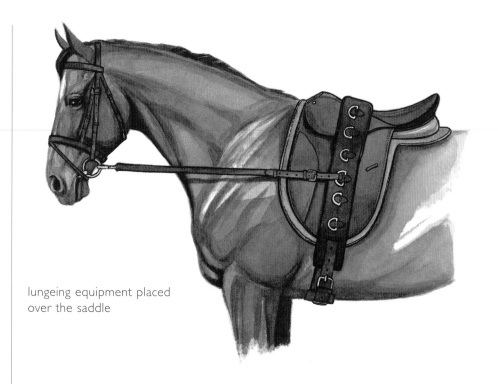

lungeing equipment placed
over the saddle

LUNGEING CAVESSONS

It is most important that the lunge cavesson should fit the head well and
not twist as the rein is used. Depending on which style you choose, there
should be a strap on the cheek of a cavesson that enables you to secure
the cheek well back from the horse's eye. If a throatlatch is also fitted this
should be loose to allow the horse to flex his head without pressure on the
throat. The nosepiece will take most of the pressure so it should be strong
and well padded. The centre ring should be strong and on a swivel and
any additional side rings should be secure to allow side reins to be fitted
if necessary. In original patterns of lungeing cavessons, these side rings
were more correctly placed on the nosepiece just under the cheekpiece
and therefore in a better and more useful position for attaching side reins.

Young Horses
When you work a young horse on the lunge keep the equipment simple,
take the noseband off the bridle and remove the reins if this is to be a
lunge-only session. Make sure the noseband and the throatlatch of the

lungeing cavesson fastened with the cheek pulled well back from the eye

cavesson are done up under the cheekpieces of the bridle so that no part of the bridle digs into the horse's face and the cavesson does not interfere with the action of the bit if you have schooling equipment attached to the bit.

The Wels lungeing cavesson

This is the only cavesson that can be used as a drop noseband as well as a conventional lungeing cavesson. It is unique as the metal nosepiece has two joints, one on either side of the nose, and no joint in the centre. This makes for a much better and closer fit around the horse's nose. There is no throatlatch but a cheek strap set much lower on the cheekpiece to create a snug fit enabling the cheek to be angled well back from the eye. It is made of good quality English leather with a soft well-padded leather nosepiece.

Wels lungeing cavesson worn as a drop noseband

TO FIT The nosepiece should be fitted at the same height as a cavesson noseband, i.e. high enough not to affect the horse's breathing. The noseband should fit firmly so that the nosepiece cannot slide from side to side and the cheek strap should fit under the horse's cheek bone firmly so that the cheek of the cavesson is slightly angled back. This helps to prevent the cheeks lying uncomfortably near the horse's eye.

E. Jeffries leather cavesson

This is a traditional design and a substantially made cavesson. It has buckles on either side of the headpiece for ease of adjustment and a well-padded nosepiece with the padding extending around most of the nose. As with all leatherwork, the better the quality of leather and the better maintained it is, the softer and suppler it is next to the horse's skin.

TO FIT It is important that you get the right size of cavesson for your horse or pony. A 12 hand Welsh pony is going to find a cob-size cavesson very uncomfortable. If the nearest size available does not fit well it is possible to get your saddler to make a few adjustments in order to achieve the best fit. Again, as with all pieces of equipment fitted to the horse's nose, it should be high enough not to affect the horse's breathing and the cheeks should be firmly secured well back from the eye area.

E. Jeffries leather cavesson

Webbing cavesson

There are several designs of webbing cavesson on the market, some of them fit reasonably well, others do not. If you follow the correct principles for fitting a lunge cavesson it will become immediately apparent which fit well and will do a good job and which will be uncomfortable for the horse, will move on the face and interfere with the job of successful lungeing.

TO FIT It is important that you try to achieve the best fit possible from a webbing cavesson; try to get the noseband to fit closely to the nose so that side to side movement is reduced to a minimum. The main fault with these cavessons is they do tend to be very large around the nose and twist round

webbing cavesson

as the lunge rein pulls the horse into a circle. Some are designed in such a way that it is difficult to secure the nosepiece of the cavesson under the cheeks of your bridle. When you have put the cavesson over your bridle you may have to undo the cheeks of the bridle and then do them up again on the outside so that the cavesson lies neatly next to your horse's face.

SIDE REINS

Side reins should not be adjusted too tightly to force a horse into a certain head carriage; this will simply make the horse tuck his head into his chest without engaging the quarters or working the back properly and the stride will become short and stilted. Once a horse has learnt to drop the contact with the bit it is very difficult to encourage him to take it up again as each time the rein is taken up the horse thinks it is correct to tuck his head in and drop the rein. You are always trying to achieve a state whereby the horse reaches forward and seeks to take up the contact.

TO FIT The side reins should not be fitted onto the bit until the horse is in the schooling area in which he is to work, and then they should be attached to the bit so that they are straight without any tension when the horse's head is in a natural and relaxed position at the halt. If you are trying to create a very long low stretch with a deep profile then the reins can be attached side by side in between the horse's front legs by being looped around the girth then up to each bit ring. To use side reins attached in

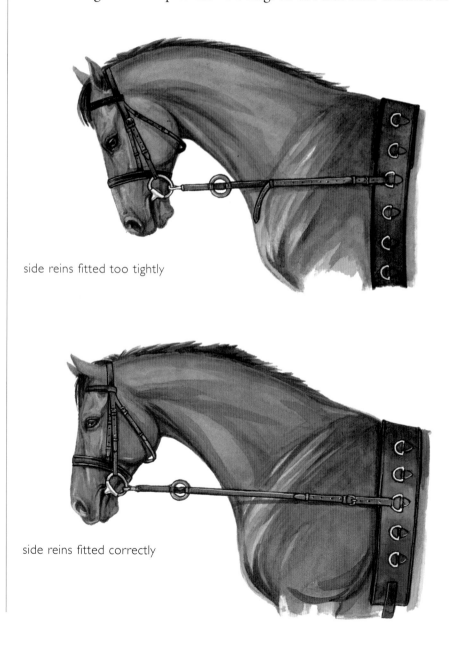

side reins fitted too tightly

side reins fitted correctly

this way is not suitable for a very young or overexuberant horse as there is always a risk of the horse catching his legs in the reins. If you want to encourage a less deep response, attach the reins to the girth straps under the saddle flap above the girth or preferably onto the side rings of a lungeing roller.

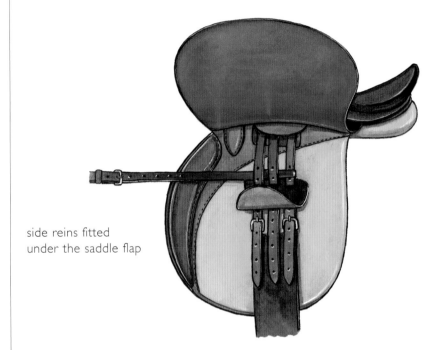

side reins fitted
under the saddle flap

Solid leather
This type of side rein has no give in it at all and is used more frequently on trained older horses rather than on young less experienced animals. Some older horses will have learned to lean on elasticated side reins to test the strength of them.

Leather with an elastic insert
Made of good quality leather like the solid leather side reins, but these incorporate an elastic insert to provide more give as the horse is worked.

Leather with a rubber ring insert
These side reins have a rubber ring insert with a piece of leather continuing behind the ring to prevent it stretching too far.

Leather with a snubber
The same principal applies to these side reins but, instead of a piece of elastic material, a strong rubber snubber is used. The snubber is actually so substantial that it has very little give if any at all.

Nylon with an elastic insert
This is the least expensive form of side rein. It is not as easy to ensure that these reins are of the same length as they are fastened by a rocko buckle (sliding buckle) instead of a conventional buckle with a tongue that fits into specific holes thus making equal adjustment easier. In addition, they are usually quite short so are not suitable for large horses as they cannot be adjusted to comfortably accommodate longer necks.

solid leather

leather with an elastic insert

leather with a rubber ring insert

leather with a snubber

nylon with an elastic insert

LUNGE REINS

Lunge reins or lines should be strong, well made and thick enough for the trainer to hold properly. Cotton-based webs or cushioned webs are best because in times of crisis when strength is needed, the rein does not slip through the trainer's hand or cause friction burns as some materials can, even through a pair of gloves.

The fastening should ideally be buckled leather with a swivel just below the buckle so that the rein does not twist. If the lunge cavesson has a swivel the lunge rein does not necessarily need one as well. If the fastening is a clip then a good quality substantial trigger clip is best and it should also have a swivel just below the trigger. Nothing is more dangerous or frightening than a strong horse suddenly escaping as the clip on your lunge line gives way under the strain.

It is very important that the lunge rein is a suitable length for the size of horse being lunged. The usual length of standard reins available in tack shops is 21 ft or sometimes 24 ft. These lengths are fine for ponies or cob-size animals but for a large horse to work on the lunge without unnecessary strain on the joints, the length should be about 30 ft. This enables the horse to make a larger circle around the trainer; working on a small tight circle for any length of time is a great strain on joints and limbs, particularly the hocks.

tubular web

Tubular web

This rein is normally made in white, fairly soft cotton tubular webbing with a buckle and swivel fastening. A very traditional lunge rein but obviously anything in white is not as practical in these modern times as all the coloured cotton webs available. Also, it is not as resilient to being left out in a wet sand school as nylon!

Continental Web

These reins can be made of four-, five- or six-cord continental webbing in brown or black. This is the same material that continental reins are made from and it comes in ½ in, ⅝ in, ¾ in or 1 in thicknesses. Saddlers can buy this material by the metre and make up any length of lunge, long or draw rein that you require with whatever fastening or hand part you feel most comfortable with.

Cushioned web

This material comes in a variety of colours and is normally made up by major manufacturers in either 21 ft or 24 ft reins. It gives the handler a soft, but very substantial, flexible lunge rein to work with. Make sure the clips are good quality as this could be a potential weak spot.

Continental web
lunge line

cushioned web
lunge line

LUNGEING ROLLERS

Leather lungeing rollers

These rollers can be expensive but if they are well maintained are well worth the outlay. The best of them have a proper tree in the pad just like a driving saddle so that the tree can rest on each side of the horse's withers and there is a gap that clears the spine. The rollers usually come with a matching leather girth like a dressage girth but, if they do not, an ordinary leather dressage girth will fasten it just as safely. The more D rings on each side of the roller the better, then you have a choice of levels at which to attach various pieces of schooling equipment.

TO FIT Even with a tree in the saddle of your roller it is best to place a small pad under the roller and pull it well up into the roller's gullet to ensure that it is a comfortable fit. Girth the roller up evenly so that the buckles are at the same level on each side of your horse. It does not have to be as tight as a saddle girth but tight enough not to slip round.

Webbing lungeing rollers

This type of roller is usually sold as the roller only; you either buy a new webbing girth to fasten it or use one you already own. These do not have a rigid tree in them but are nevertheless fairly substantial and have a variety of ring options.

leather
lungeing roller

webbing
lungeing roller

3 LONG REINING

Long Reining, as with lungeing, really needs a lot of patient practice; you cannot afford to make mistakes, particularly with a young horse. Unlike lungeing, when the rein is attached to the nosepiece and if the horse moves more quickly than anticipated the worst that can happen will be a strong pull on the cavesson, if you make a mistake while long reining, when you are normally attached directly to the horse's mouth, at best you will jab the horse in the mouth and at worst you can actually damage and bruise the bars and the tongue.

The main reasons for long reining are:
• to teach a young horse to move forward
  confidently;
• to mouth a young horse;
• to improve the horse's balance;
• to improve the horse's carriage and gaits;
• more progressive training of schooled horses;
• the training of High School movements.

There are several methods of long reining and a few particularly good books on the merits of each method and how to do it. You will need to decide which method is most suitable for you and the work programme you have decided on. If you decide on a method that involves long reining from behind your horse then you will need to be very fit and fairly fast as continuous trotting is very tiring! You also need to consider the equipment you use as each method involves different distances between horse and handler and different heights at which the reins are attached to the horse. The length of your reins in particular will need consideration; reins for the

training on long reins

English method, for instance, which involves circle work, may be too long for close work and leave you with a lot of spare rein to hold.

Suitable bits

The most comfortable bits for long reining are half spoon or D ring snaffles as the actual cheek of the bit helps the horse to turn by supporting the signals each rein makes. Also, using a cheeked bit eliminates the chance of pulling the bit through the horse's mouth. The half-spoon snaffle has a cheek at the bottom so that the cheek lies neatly below the face which makes it less likely to be caught up in any other piece of equipment.

half spoon
jointed snaffle

D ring
jointed snaffle

LONG REINS

The length of your long reins depends on which method of long reining you adopt. If you are going to, in effect, lunge your horse on two reins for most of the work on long reins, then lunge rein lengths will apply: 21–24 ft for ponies and cobs and 30–36 ft for larger horses as you will need to use the full width of a school in order not to put too much strain on the horse while circling continuously. If you are driving your horse on long reins by walking behind, then very long reins may be difficult to manage safely.

Material

The material that your long reins are made up of is really entirely up to individual preference. Tubular cotton webbing, cushion webbing and Continental webbing, are all very suitable. Make sure you get the right thickness of rein for the size of your hands, too thick or too thin can mean that your ability to hold the reins sensitively and effectively will be impaired if you are struggling to hold both reins and your whip. Some people favour soft flexible plough lines as long reins, though these are not as easy to buy and are sometimes too short for large horses.

LONG-REINING ROLLERS

You need a substantial roller if you are going to do a significant amount of long reining. A well-maintained leather roller is best and well worth the outlay but they do cost a lot of money. One or more pairs of terrets either side at the top of the roller are very useful and then a series of at least four D rings on each side is also very useful. If you are going to use the top pair of terrets to put your long reins through you need to position yourself nearer to the horse's quarters than to the shoulder when lunge/long reining, as it is very easy for the

long reining roller complete with terrets and D rings

horse to turn towards you and as soon as the reins wrap around the terrets of the roller you lose the ability to guide the horse.

Cruppers

Using a crupper helps to stabilise your roller and keep it more secure on the horse's back. If your horse is not used to a crupper, introduce it in the stable in a controlled environment so that the horse has time to familiarise himself with the feel of it before you work him outside. Your roller will need an additional D ring at the back of the pad on the top for the attachment of the crupper. It is very important that the dock part of the crupper is kept very supple as the skin under the horse's tail is very sensitive and can be rubbed very easily; keep a careful check on this area.

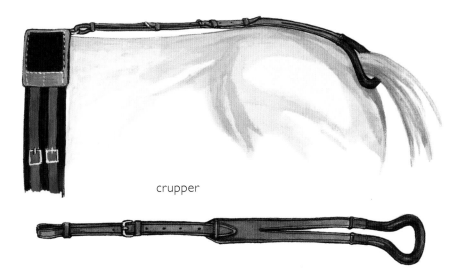

crupper

4 LAUFER OR SLIDING SIDE REINS

L AUFER OR SLIDING SIDE reins are one of the most useful items of schooling equipment and can be used either in ridden, lunge or driven schooling. They encourage the horse to find his own balance, accept bit pressure and acquire a comfortable profile in all gaits. As the name suggests the contact is a sliding one with the horse's mouth, there is no forcing of the outline; the horse can alter his profile to comfortably suit the gait. The horse's profile and level of head carriage changes as the gaits change. If you use a piece of schooling equipment that relies on fixing a position, this can mean that the horse is not as comfortable in all the gaits. With Laufer reins, the only real resistance is felt when the head carriage is taken very high or

the horse working in Laufer or sliding side reins

the nose is poked too far forward, the horse then feels a strong downward pressure on the bars of the mouth which should encourage him to lower his head and bring his nose back to the vertical. Laufer reins, like all pieces of schooling equipment, rely on the rider or driver maintaining a steady degree of forward movement; it is not enough to put on a device and then let the horse slop around or, alternatively, move too fast and compromise good balance.

TO FIT Laufer reins either fit to the top ring of a lungeing roller or to the top of a driving pad or to the top Ds of a saddle, then run along each side of the horse's neck, passing from the inside to the outside of the bit ring. They then go either down between the horse's front legs, threaded through the girth for a deeper profile, or along the horse's side to fasten under the flap of the saddle in the manner of side reins or to the bottom ring of a lungeing roller or just above the girth on a driving pad. As a general guide, when the horse is standing in a relaxed position at the halt the sliding side reins should be adjusted so that the reins are just taut without drawing the horse's head in or pulling on the bars of the mouth.

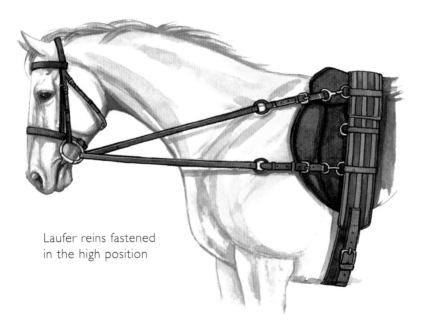

Laufer reins fastened
in the high position

5 THE CHAMBON

THE CHAMBON IS A TRAINING AID designed to be used on the lunge or for loose schooling sessions. It is a very useful training aid for slow, careful, rhythmic trot work on the lunge with a horse that needs to be encouraged to take a longer, lower profile. It helps to engage the hindquarters and build the muscles of the horse's topline. It encourages the horse to lower his head but does not ask for any flexion at the poll. The horse learns to drop his head and carry the head and neck low and extended but, as no

the Chambon
correctly fitted

flexion is asked for and there is no lateral support, the nose is still able to poke out at the front. A very useful training aid for a horse with a weak back or a horse that through wrong schooling has built up the underside of the neck. The Chambon works the hindquarters very thoroughly so care must be taken not to work the horse for too long in it especially in the early introductory stages as he will become tired and uncomfortable very quickly. It should then be adjusted gradually so that the device can only be felt if the horse tries to lift his head too high and hollow the back; he quickly learns to lower his head and neck and adopt a comfortable working profile. So with care and regular short sessions a horse with, say, a ewe neck and a weak topline is gradually encouraged to lower the profile and the topline muscles are strengthened and built up so that the horse eventually only finds it natural and comfortable to adopt a lower more relaxed way of going.

TO FIT The Chambon should not be put on until the horse is in the work space and then it should be attached loosely at first while the horse warms up and gets accustomed to the feel of the aid. It is attached to the girth by an adjustable leather loop which passes up between the horse's front legs, this divides at the chest into two pieces of cord that pass up either side of the underneck to two little pulleys on either side of a padded headpiece attached to the top of the bridle. The cords then run down either side of the horse's face and fasten to each snaffle bit ring.

the horse working
very low in a
Chambon

6 THE DE GOGUE

T HE DE GOGUE CAN BE SAID to be a variation of the Chambon but, where the Chambon is only designed to be used on the lunge or in loose schooling work, the de Gogue can be used for ridden work as well. It has a similar action of encouraging the horse to lower his head and extend his neck. However, the fact that the cord which passes down the horse's face from the pollpiece does not attach to the bit ring but passes through it and

the de Gogue

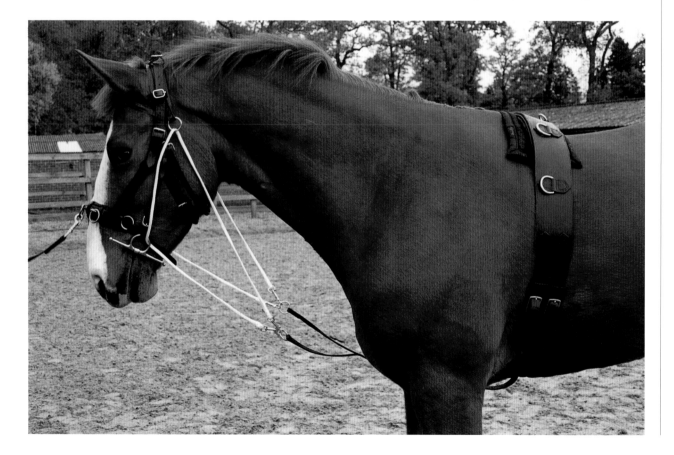

back down to the centre of the chest where it clips on to metal loops, means that a certain degree of poll action is asked for, thus encouraging the horse not only to seek a longer, lower profile but to bring the face into a balanced vertical profile.

TO FIT The de Gogue is attached to the girth by an adjustable leather loop which passes up between the horse's front legs. This divides at the chest into two pieces of cord that pass up either side of the underneck to two little pulleys on either side of a padded headpiece attached to the top of the bridle. The cords then run down either side of the horse's face and pass through the bit rings of the snaffle. If lungeing, the cords then pass back down to a D ring on the martingale piece at the horse's chest. When the horse is being ridden, the cords, after passing through the rings of the snaffle, go to the rider's hands alongside the riding reins.

being ridden in a
de Gogue

7 THE ABBOT DAVIS BALANCING REIN

THE ABBOT DAVIES BALANCING REIN is a system of schooling the horse to the correct balance and creating a relaxed profile thus enabling the horse to build up back and topline muscles. The system is used in three different positions and encourages the neck to lower and stretch and engages the quarters. The main aim of the system is to build up a correct profile so that the horse automatically finds it more natural and comfortable to move and work in the correct shape in an ordinary snaffle bit. The system works on the principles of pulleys and levers and also uses the age-old training method of using the tail: the tail is pulled between the horse's hind legs and then attached to the training rein that goes up to the mouth.

TO FIT Quite a substantial amount of equipment is involved in this system so following the instructions provided to use and fit this is essential. A complete booklet is provided with this training aid at point of sale.

The three positions are:
1. attached from the mouth to the girth;
2. attached from the mouth to the tail with a rope;
3. attached from the mouth to behind the ears with a rubber connecter.

Abbot Davies Balancing Rein

Abbot Davies Balancing Rein: position 1

Abbot Davies Balancing Rein: position 2

Abbot Davies Balancing
Rein: position 3

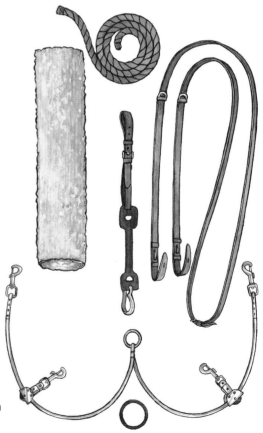

the pieces which make up the
Abbot Davies Balancing system

8 THE NATHE COMBI TRAINER

THE NATHE COMBI TRAINER IS DESIGNED to be used on the lunge. It is a very simple but effective schooling device requiring very little additional equipment to be used in conjunction with it. It is basically driving-harness breeching that extends either side of the horse's body and attaches to the bit rings. It is adjusted on the loin straps and along the trace line. The trainer is made of 1in nylon webbing with a protective plastic sleeve on the breeching to prevent friction rubbing and, at the bit end, the

working in a Nathe Combi trainer

last 24 in is thick elastic. It encourages a low, relaxed profile and the breeching helps to encourage the horse to engage the quarters. When the head is raised and the nose extended, the breeching tightens on the quarters and there is a downward pull on the bars of the mouth. As the head drops and the hind legs step further under the body the tension is relaxed. This is a device that positively encourages low, powerful forward movement.

TO FIT A horse accustomed to wearing breeching will not notice any difference in wearing this equipment from wearing driving harness but great care must be taken when introducing this piece of equipment to a horse that is not. The Nathe Combi trainer should not be attached to the bit until the horse is ready to work in the lungeing area. It should be adjusted to accommodate a long profile so that it is just straight when the horse is standing still with his head in a natural and relaxed position. When the horse is worked in and relaxed then the Nathe Combi trainer can be adjusted so that the head is just in front of the vertical. It is very important that this equipment is adjusted correctly, it must not be over-shortened and make the horse overbend.

9 THE PESSOA TRAINING SYSTEM

T HE PESSOA TRAINING SYSTEM is designed to work the horse in four different positions encouraging balance and a gradual build-up of muscle along the horse's topline, providing the person using the equipment lunges the horse well and in a controlled forward manner. The horse should be encouraged to engage the quarters as the system works on the principle of pulleys and levers. If the horse resists by lifting the head and the nose, there is pressure on the bars of the mouth and the hindquarters. As soon as the horse drops his head or gives with the head and jaw, the pressure is alleviated.

working in the low position Pessoa

TO FIT There is quite a lot of equipment to be fitted to the horse so the instructions given with each Pessoa training aid should be followed care-fully. This equipment also relies on breeching so, again, if your horse is not accustomed to wearing harness, introduce this part of the equipment carefully in a controlled environment. This is a potentially powerful piece of equipment so gradual introduction and short but correct initial sessions will get better results.

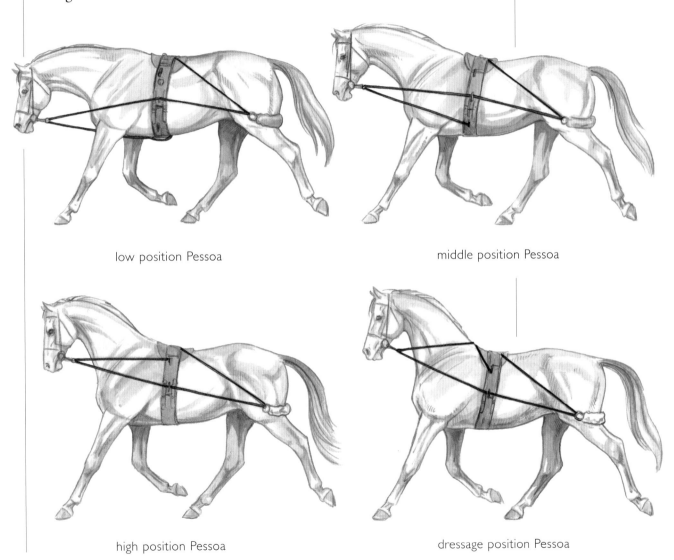

low position Pessoa

middle position Pessoa

high position Pessoa

dressage position Pessoa

10 THE MARKET HARBOROUGH

THE MARKET HARBOROUGH IS A combination of a static rein attached to a snaffle bit and a draw rein. The draw rein looks very similar to a martingale. It is looped around the girth, runs between the horse's front legs, up through a neckstrap, divides, passing through each bit ring from inside to outside, and then clips onto a series of spaced D rings on the reins. As the rein is pulled, the draw rein slides over the top rein and, depending on how tightly it is adjusted, it draws the horse's nose in. The

working in a Market Harborough

draw rein is only brought to bear when the horse carries his head too high or throws it up; it should, therefore, be adjusted so as not to be restrictive when the head is at a normal angle. It has been used very successfully by trainers teaching riders to experience the feel of a horse in a more rounded profile while they are working on becoming more effective with leg aids.

TO FIT The neck strap and girth loop are fitted as an ordinary martingale would be. The draw rein should pass through the bit rings from inside to outside and should be adjusted so that, when the reins take effect, the horse's nose is pulled only to the vertical position and not into the chest.

11 THE HALSVERLENGER

HALSVERLENGER MEANS neck stretcher. This piece of equipment can be used for either ridden or lunge work. It is a strong piece of elastic with a woven nylon sleeve covering it; it has two clips at each end and is passed through a plastic block so that the rein is equally divided into two. It is designed to encourage the horse to bring his nose into a horizontal position by a combination of poll pressure and pressure on the bars of the mouth independently of the rider's hand.

the Halsverlenger used for either ridden or lunge work

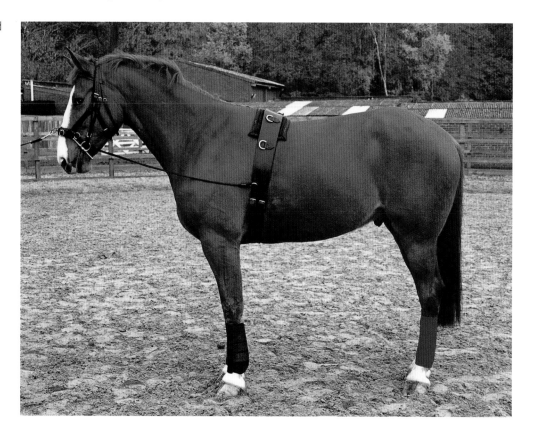

THE HALSVERLENGER

TO FIT The block sits on top of the horse's head and both reins are passed down the sides of the horse's face and through the snaffle bit rings from outside to inside, then they run alongside the shoulders on either side of the horse and are attached to either a lunging roller or the girth of a saddle. If a deeper profile is required, the reins pass from the bit rings down the horse's chest, through the horse's front legs and are attached to the girth. Pulling the elastic through the block and forming a loop on top of the horse's head makes adjustments to the overall length. This device is not always long enough for larger horses but you can extend it by putting a loop of leather around the girth then clipping the Halsverlenger to the loop.

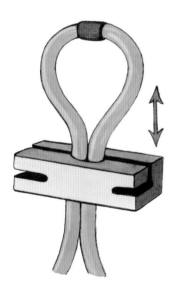

Halsverlenger poll-fitting
as you pull it up

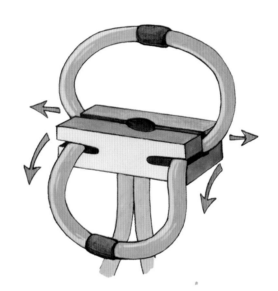

Halsverlenger secured
into poll-fitting

12 DRAW REINS

DRAW REINS ARE ONE PIECE of schooling equipment that is most often seen in a wide variety of equestrian disciplines. They are used only for ridden schooling and always with a second rein acting just on the bit; draw reins are never used by themselves. Standard draw reins should be 16 ft long (each rein is 8 ft) and come in several designs. Riders wishing to work-in with them prior to a competition, then remove them quickly before going

draw reins are used in ridden schooling

into the ring, need to use a pattern that comes with separate loops (either a single loop or two loops). The girth is passed through the loops and the draw reins clip to metal Ds on the loops. This makes it easy to remove them without having to undo the girth. Polo draw reins, which are not removed before play, should have substantial sewn loops that attach directly to the girth because great pressure is brought to bear during play and a clip is a potential weak spot.

Where you position the reins depends on what sort of profile you are trying to achieve. If a very deep head and neck position is sought then the reins need to be attached to the girth and run between the horse's front legs. If you wish to just tip the horse's nose in without dropping the head then the reins need to run along the horse's shoulder and be fastened to the girth under the saddle flap. Incorrectly used, this device will do more damage than good; it is not enough to just tip the horse's nose in by force. The idea of draw reins is to ride with a firm seat and good strong leg aids so that the horse is helped to a rounded profile by the draw reins while keeping a good supple contact with the bit and working well from behind.

TO FIT The reins can either loop around the girth coming up between the horse's front legs to the bit, passing from the inside to the outside of the bit rings, and up to the rider's hands, or they can come from the girth, attached just under the rider's legs, through the bit rings and into the rider's hands. The second method of attachment is preferable with a horse who has a tendency to rear or strike with the front feet as there is less likelihood of the feet being caught in the reins; alternatively the draw reins could be passed through a martingale neckstrap. It is important that the reins are passed from the inside to the outside of the bit because passing them from the outside to the inside would put severe pressure on the sides of the horse's face.

13 THE HARBRIDGE

THE HARBRIDGE CAN BE USED for either lunge work, loose schooling work or ridden work. Because of the low point of contact from which the device operates it encourages the horse to adopt a long low profile and a high degree of poll flexion but allows the horse freedom to bend laterally. As there is nothing for the horse to lean on he must learn to carry himself and in so doing the correct muscles are built up making it natural for the

the Harbridge is used for lunge work, loose schooling, or ridden work

horse to always work in a good shape within the limitations of his confor-mation. It is probably best used either for loose schooling or for lunge work for the first few sessions to develop a stronger musculature before the weight of a rider is added. When used for a riding lesson the Harbridge enables the instructor to demonstrate to the pupil the 'feel' they wish them to achieve without the less experienced rider having to work too hard and therefore compromising their balance and position. The Harbridge comes in two sizes, pony/cob and cob/full size.

TO FIT The Harbridge is adjustable in two places: on the actual reins themselves and also under the chest. It is easy to fit; when putting on the saddle or lungeing roller, thread the girth loop onto the girth and girth up as normal, then both reins pass between the horse's front legs and the trigger clip at the end of each rein is clipped to each bit ring. It should only be clipped into place when in the school or as you are about to ride off, the horse should never be led to the school with equipment already attached. As with any new piece of equipment or schooling device, the Harbridge should be introduced gradually as muscles unaccustomed to working in certain shapes soon tire and the horse will begin to resist and spoil the effect you are trying to create.

14 THE SCHOOLMASTA TRAINING AID

THE SCHOOLMASTA IS A VARIATION of high-fitting side reins and is used for ridden schooling; the reins are fixed in a high position on the top of the horse's withers. It consists of a specially designed and strengthened numnah with a D ring just in front of the pommel of the saddle. A trigger clip fastens to this D which has a pulley attached to it to allow a cord to run freely through the pulley. Attached to each end of the cord are two solid leather side reins that run down each side of the horse's neck to the bit. Although the action of this training aid is the same as high, fixed side reins, the free-running cord at the saddle end gives the horse a lot of

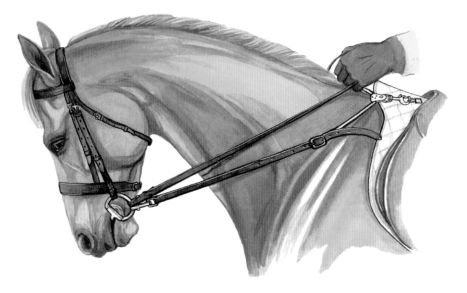

the Schoolmasta training aid is used for ridden schooling

lateral freedom. This encourages the horse to maintain a stable head carriage while allowing for turning and small-circle work without compromising forward movement.

TO FIT Fit the numnah under the saddle pulling it well up into the gullet of the saddle. Before you do the girth up, make sure it is far enough forward so that the D ring is well clear of the pommel. Clip the trigger clip onto the D ring on the numnah just in front of the horse's wither. Adjust the side reins so that they are straight when the horse's head is in a relaxed position at the halt. As with all training aids, introduce the Schoolmasta gradually allowing the horse freedom to hold himself naturally and do not shorten it so that the horse is tied down into a position that cannot possibly be maintained for any length of time.

15 THE EQUILONGE

THE EQUILONGE CAN BE USED FOR lunge work or ridden work. It has a broad pollpiece that sits behind the headpiece of the bridle which joins two rolled cheekpieces that run down the sides of the horse's face. On the cheekpieces there are two pulley clips attached to two pieces of cord, these run down to a leather strap that attaches to the girth between the horse's front legs. The end of the cheekpieces clip to the snaffle rings of

the Equilonge is for lunge work or ridden work

the bit. If the horse raises his head too high, the rein tightens from the chest to the poll putting pressure on the top of the poll and on the bars of the mouth; as soon as the head drops into a more relaxed position, pressure is immediately released. If the horse pulls or pokes his nose out in front, the rein tightens from the chest putting pressure on the bars of the mouth. As soon as the nose relaxes and drops to the vertical the pressure is released again. As with any device attached only to the forehand, the effectiveness of the Equilonge relies very much on the person controlling the horse to keep good controlled forward movement and create activity from the hind legs.

TO FIT The headpiece of the Equilonge fits just behind the headpiece of the bridle and is fastened by a small piece of buckled leather. Two rolled pieces of leather are attached to the pollpiece, run down either side of the horse's face and extend below the horse's chin ending in two metal loops. On the rolled leather cheeks are two pulley clips, the rolled leather runs through the pulley and the clip end is clipped to the back of the snaffle bit. Two pieces of cord run up the horse's chest from a loop attached to the girth and are threaded through the end of the metal loops that come down from the rolled cheekpieces.

16 MARTINGALES

Running martingale

A running martingale is designed to prevent the horse lifting his head too high, and therefore out of the angle of control. This device relies on the correct tension of the reins to maintain control over the head. Attached to the girth it passes up between the horse's front legs and divides at the upper chest, each strap end has a ring on it through which the reins pass. So that the martingale strap does not hang down and possibly interfere with the horse's front legs, the strap is held in position by a neck strap. A rubber martingale stop should be fitted to prevent the neckstrap sliding up and down the actual martingale, and rein stops should be fitted to each rein to prevent the rings of the martingale getting hooked up where the reins join the bit.

running martingale

TO FIT Correctly fitted, a running martingale should only take effect when the head is raised very high and/or the head becomes difficult to control, if it is too short there will be a constant downward pressure on the bars of the mouth. A guide to the correct length when the martingale is in place but not yet attached to the reins is that you should be able to take the straps that attach to the reins to one side and stretch the straps as far as the horse's withers.

Standing martingale

This is also designed to prevent the horse's head from getting too high, and therefore difficult for the rider to control, but instead of relying on pressure on the horse's mouth it puts pressure on the nose. This device should only be secured to a cavesson noseband or the cavesson part of a flash noseband and never to the dropped part of any other noseband. The martingale is attached to the girth between the horse's front legs at one end and to the back of a cavesson noseband at the other end. Again, as with the running version, to prevent the martingale strap from dropping dangerously low between the horse's front legs it passes through a neck strap, which should be fitted with a martingale stop, to hold it in place.

standing martingale attached to a noseband

TO FIT When the martingale is on the horse, place a hand below the martingale strap between the noseband and the neck strap; if you can lift the martingale strap into the angle of the horse's throat it is the correct length.

Cheshire martingale

This martingale is rarely seen these days. It is a combination of a hunting breastplate and the type of standing martingale that attaches to the bit. It applies downward pressure on the bars of the mouth if the horse's head is raised very high.

TO FIT The breastplate should be fitted so that three fingers width can be placed between the neck strap and the horse's neck and a further three fingers width between the horse's chest and the strap that runs from the girth to the neck strap. The martingale straps between the chest and the mouth should be long enough so that, when attached to the bit, the straps if pulled up will reach into the angle of the horse's throat, as with the fitting of a standing martingale. At the bit end the martingale straps should be attached below the reins not above so that they will not interfere with the action of the reins.

Cheshire martingale

Polo martingale

This is a standing martingale that is reinforced with chrome leather all along the martingale strap that runs from the horse's chest to the noseband. Polo is a fast and vigorous contact sport and all the equipment needs to be very substantially made. The polo martingale also has the length adjustment between the neckstrap and the noseband (unlike a normal standing martingale which is adjusted between the horse's front legs) to enable quick adjustments to be carried out.

TO FIT It is normally fitted a little tighter than a standard standing martingale but care should be taken not to overshorten the martingale because the polo pony needs his head and neck for balance when making fast turns and halts.

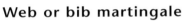

polo martingale

Web or bib martingale

Designed to fill the dual role of running and Irish martingales, this looks just like a running martingale but a solid piece of leather is sewn into the V made by the rein attachments. This acts like a running martingale, pulling down on the bars of the mouth if the head is thrown up or carried too high. Also, if the rider is thrown, the bib piece helps to prevent the reins being thrown over the horse's head and getting caught up in the front feet.

TO FIT The fitting of the web or bib martingale is the same as a running martingale and the effect on the horse will be the same as that of an ordinary running martingale. The immobility of the solid leather part keeps the reins in place fairly close together. This part needs to be kept very supple or it can rub the underside of the horse's neck.

web or bib martingale

Irish martingale

The Irish martingale is designed to stop the reins from going over the horse's head in the event of the rider coming off and is most commonly seen on racehorses. It is made up of two rings joined by a leather or web strap approximately 4 in long.

TO FIT The reins are threaded through the rings and the martingale keeps the reins in place just under the horse's neck. This piece of equipment should always have martingale stops fitted to each rein so that the rings do not get caught up on the buckle or billet fastenings of the reins where they attach to the bit.

Combination martingale

This is a blend of both standing and running martingales. It is basically a running martingale but, where the straps divide, there is an extra ring to which is attached a standing martingale piece.

TO FIT The combination is fitted as a running martingale, with the standing part adjusted to act only if the horse's head is thrown right up above the height that the running part can control. When used on a jumping horse, great care must be taken to ensure that the standing part is correctly fitted so that the horse has enough freedom to jump well.

Tandem martingale

The tandem is a running martingale that, instead of having just one ring at the point were the martingale attaches to the reins, has a two-point contact. The straps forming the V of the martingale are attached to metal pieces that enable the reins to run through two rings 6 in apart so, instead of the rein being pulled down at one fixed point, the load is spread over a wider area; the idea is that the downward drag on the bars of the mouth is not quite so severe. This also comes with extra rings so that it can be turned into a conventional running martingale.

TO FIT Fit the tandem like a normal running martingale but pay special attention to the metal pieces to ensure they do not rub the hair of the horse's neck.

Irish martingale

combination
martingale

tandem martingale

17 NOSEBANDS

Cavesson noseband

In its most simple form the cavesson is just a straight band around the horse's nose attached by a sliphead to the bridle. Different widths can be used to good effect: a thin or a rolled nosepiece will suit a very fine delicate head, whereas a thick nosepiece on a long face can give the impression of a much shorter head. A thick band strategically placed can improve a nose with a bump in the wrong place.

TO FIT If fitted for only cosmetic effect, the band should lie two finger widths below the projecting cheekbone and you should be able to get two fingers between the band and the nose. Fitted a little lower and fastened tighter, the cavesson can discourage the horse from opening his mouth too

cavesson
noseband

wide to evade the action of the bit, in this case a thicker padded band should be used to distribute the pressure more evenly.

Crank noseband

This noseband has several different names and slight variations of style but the principle is the same. The band is well padded because it has to be tight to be effective so you must ensure that it fits the horse well. The strapping actually doubles back on itself enabling it to be tightened potentially very severely. When circumstances dictate that a flash or drop noseband cannot be used, for instance with a double bridle, this noseband firmly fastened will help to dissuade the horse from opening his mouth to evade the action of the bit.

crank noseband

TO FIT It should be fitted like a cavesson noseband. The padding should almost meet when the noseband is done up to the required tightness, so that the thinner, non-padded tightening strap does not touch the horse. Extra padding can be put behind the noseband where the pressure is greatest to prevent rubbing.

Flash noseband

The flash is really a cavesson with a detachable lower strap. The noseband was designed to allow a standing martingale to be fitted to the cavesson part if required, the lower strap can be fitted quite tightly to dissuade a horse from opening his mouth too wide.

TO FIT Although fitted just like a cavesson, it should be high enough to ensure that the lower strap does not interfere with the horse's breathing. For the noseband to have any effect, both bands must be fastened quite tightly. If you are relying on a tight noseband every time you ride you must make sure that the horse is not getting rubs or calluses from the constant pressure. The lower strap should be done up on the side of the nose and not directly under the chin, this is much more comfortable for the horse.

flash noseband

Drop noseband

If fitted correctly the drop noseband closes the mouth more effectively than any other aid. As the horse opens his mouth to evade, a lot of nose pressure is created, this encourages the horse to drop his nose and relax his jaw to relieve the pressure. Care must be taken in the fitting of the drop; I have always had drop nosebands specially made. The ones usually available in tack shops are too long at the front of the nose and the buckle end of the back strap can often also be too long and the strap end too short, making it impossible to fit correctly. The best 'shop bought' ones are of the fully adjustable style that can be altered either side of the nose.

TO FIT The drop should be fitted with the front of the band above the nostrils on the solid part of the nose and not on the soft, fleshy nasal cartilage, the back strap should angle down below the bit and do up between the chin groove and the corner of the mouth, to avoid any pinching.

drop noseband

Grakle noseband

This is an effective aid for upper and lower jaw pressure working on a larger overall area than a lot of other nosebands but it is not accepted by all equestrian disciplines. There are several different patterns of Grakle: the only one that works as originally intended is the one that adjusts on the nose (the straps can be moved through the nosepiece and are not riveted into place). By moving the straps through the nosepiece you are able to alter the pressure of the noseband up and down the face.

TO FIT The top strap should be fitted high, pulled up by the sliphead of the noseband but not high enough to be able to rub the projecting cheekbone; the bottom strap should slant down to fit below the bit and fasten on the side of the horse's nose, like the lower flash noseband strap, not under the chin where it may pinch.

Kineton noseband

This noseband gives quite severe nose pressure. As the bit is pulled back in the mouth, some of the pressure is transferred to the nose by the noseband pulling across and down on the nose. This often works because the formative training of young horses relies solely on pressure on the nose. There are several patterns of Kineton on the market, one allows for extra adjustment on the nosepiece itself. The original Kineton pattern had a piece of metal set into the nosepiece for more severe pressure. The metal loops fit inside and under each side of the bit and attach to the nosepiece. This noseband should only be used with a snaffle bit.

TO FIT Fitted as a drop noseband, the nosepiece should lie on the nose bone not on the nostrils. The metal loops fit inside the bit rings and under the bit mouthpiece on either side of the bit.

Grakle noseband

Kineton noseband

Bucephalus noseband

Below are two versions of the same principle: as the bit is used, the nose-band is pulled back against the front of the horse's nose and the horse feels encircling nose pressure as well as pressure from the bit both inside the mouth and in the chin groove, in the case of a bit with a curb chain.

TO FIT Both versions are normally secured to the middle of a cavesson noseband with a small strap, the Bucephalus noseband then lies on the horse's face and the straps go below the bit crossing over under the chin and hook onto the curb hooks of the bit. A version with hooks can also be hooked to the floating rings on a Wilson snaffle or into the top eye of a pelham or curb bit.

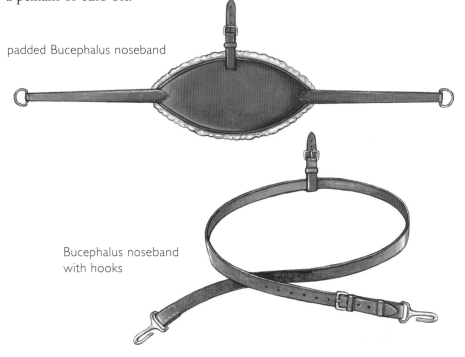

padded Bucephalus noseband

Bucephalus noseband
with hooks

Worcester noseband

The Worcester has been specifically designed to allow the rider to apply varying degrees of nose pressure by using the reins. It is a wide, padded cavesson noseband with a crank-style fastening enabling the nosepiece to be fastened very firmly thus dissuading the horse from opening his mouth very wide to evade the action of the bit. On the front of the band is an additional nosepiece sewn in two sections that angle down and fasten onto the front of each side of the bit, these straps can be adjusted to enable more or less nose pressure to be brought to bear. It also seems to encourage the horse to drop the nose to a certain extent.

TO FIT The Worcester fits like a conventional cavesson noseband, the nosepiece lying on the horse's face two finger widths below the projecting cheekbone but no lower as the drop section must obviously not interfere with the horse's breathing.

Cross-chain noseband

This is a very severe noseband which can be used on a strong horse to good effect by a very experienced rider. The action dissuades the horse from opening his mouth wide and, in particular, from crossing the jaw. As the horse tries to open his mouth to resist, there is very considerable pressure from the crossed chains on the back of the jaw. The only way the horse can alleviate this pressure is by closing the jaw and dropping the nose.

TO FIT Although this noseband looks like a drop nosepiece at the front, it should be fitted above the bit with the two chains crossed at the back of the jaw and fastened snugly but not overly tight.

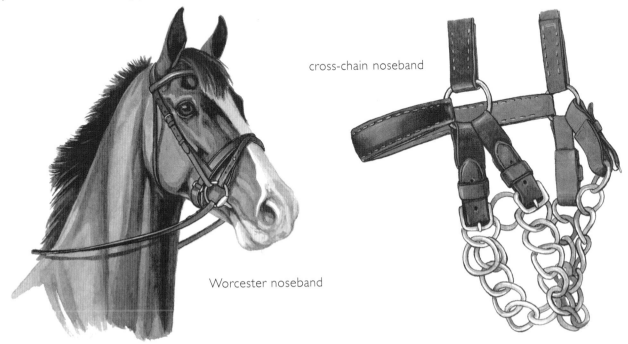

cross-chain noseband

Worcester noseband

Scawbrigg noseband

This thickly padded nosepiece adjusts on the front of the nose and the shape is similar to an adjustable drop noseband. A chinpiece passes through two rings at the back of the nosepiece and at each end of the chinpiece are rings for the reins. This can be used as a bitless bridle or you can use a combination of bit and rein by attaching the Scawbrigg to a bradoon sliphead on a conventional bridle and then attaching the bit to the cheeks of the bridle. With a rein on the bit and a rein on the Scawbrigg the rider can apply bit and nose pressure in varying degrees.

Scawbrigg noseband

TO FIT Using a conventional bridle, the Scawbrigg should be fitted high enough so that the nosepiece does not interfere with the horse's breathing and adjusted so that it fits snugly against the face before the reins are taken up. When used with a bit the nosepiece should be attached to a bradoon sliphead and the bit should be attached to the cheekpieces of the bridle. Fitted in this way, both the noseband and the bit have separate reins and the rider uses a combination of nose and bit pressure to maintain control.

Gloster noseband

The Gloster noseband can be used in five different ways to achieve very specific results. The noseband is a cavesson with a padded lower nosepiece incorporating a sprung steel core sewn into the nosepiece front. The lower piece has an encircling design with rings to which to attach a pair of reins.

1. For a horse who carries his head very high or has a tendency to rear, a standing martingale can be attached to the bottom nosepiece rings. As the horse raises his head or tries to rear, the nosepiece is tightened by the martingale and creates nose pressure, the pressure continues until the head comes back to the vertical – an easier angle of control – when the pressure is released immediately.

2. When riding reins are attached to the bit, draw reins can be attached to the lower rings applying nose pressure on the lower part of the nose. Skilful application will allow a rider to use the two sets of reins independently or to work the horse between them.

3. A neck strap can be attached to the lower nosepiece and fastened firmly around the upper neck about two hands breadth behind the ears. This helps to dissuade the horse from trying to lower his head to buck. If the head is lowered, pressure is brought to bear on the back of the upper neck and also on the lower nose, as soon as the head is raised the pressure is released.

4. If for some reason no bit is required, the headpiece of the noseband can be slipped off and the noseband can be fitted to a conventional bridle headstall, the reins then attach to the lower rings and you have a bitless bridle.

5. It can be used with two sets of reins so that one set of reins is attached to the bit and a second set is attached to the lower rings so that the horse can be worked between the two reins creating more or less nose pressure as required.

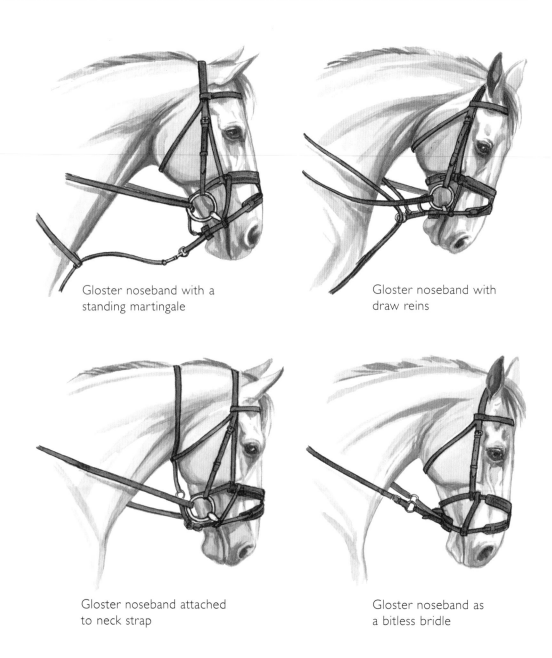

Gloster noseband with a
standing martingale

Gloster noseband with
draw reins

Gloster noseband attached
to neck strap

Gloster noseband as
a bitless bridle

TO FIT The Gloster is fitted like a cavesson noseband well up on the face but not rubbing the projecting cheekbone. The lower nosepiece is adjusted to lie on the nose bone, not on the soft fleshy nostrils, so that it does not interfere with the horse's breathing; it is fastened firmly below the bit but not overly tight. The supporting straps between the upper and lower bands should be adjusted to lie on the horse's face in front of the bit. The rein rings hang below the lower nosepiece to have either reins, draw reins, martingale or neck strap attached to them.

Combination noseband

This noseband has a short front piece attached to a curved metal cheek and two straps at the back, one lying on the upper part of the jawbone and the other lying in the curb groove. The best pattern has an adjustable front. It has very definite jaw closing qualities. As the horse resists by trying to open the mouth or cross the jaw, great pressure is felt both in the curb groove and also on the more sensitive upper jaw area. As the horse lowers his head and closes his mouth, pressure ceases, thus dissuading the horse from trying to constantly open his mouth to evade the action of the bit.

TO FIT The front nosepiece should fit at the level of a drop noseband, on the nose above the nostrils, without interfering with the horse's breathing. The upper back strap should be fastened so that you can just get one finger between the face and the band. The lower strap fastens below the bit and, again, you should be able to fit one finger's width between the strap and the horse's jaw.

combination noseband

18 COMBINATION BRIDLES

The Norton or Citation

This bridle has two mouthpieces: a loose-ring, thin wire jointed overcheck and a loose-ring jointed bradoon. The cheekpieces of the bridle attach to the rings of an overcheck. The reins attach to the rings of the bradoon. Around the mouthpiece of the overcheck are two metal fixtures that carry a nosepiece. This is a severe bridle combining very thin snaffle mouthpieces with nose and poll pressure. As the reins are used, the cheeks of the overcheck are pushed into the horse's face and the joint is forced up into the roof of the mouth. The more the bradoon pulls back in the mouth the more pressure is brought to bear on the nose and the corners of the mouth.

Norton or
Citation

TO FIT The bits must be high enough in the corners of the mouth to just cause a wrinkle and you should be able to place your index finger on each side of the horse's face between the corner of the lips and the bit rings. The nosepiece should be snug against the horse's nose, without pulling the bits forward in the mouth, and fitted as high as possible so as too interfere as little as possible with the horse's breathing. A face strap runs down the horse's face, divides, and supports the noseband at the height at which a drop noseband should be fitted.

The Newmarket

The Newmarket usually has a Wilson snaffle with a mullen or jointed mouthpiece with a leather nosepiece attached to the floating rings and supported by small straps connecting to the cheekpiece of the bridle. It is used with two sets of reins so that when the snaffle rein is used the bit acts as a snaffle with the added severity of the floating rings pushing in on the sides of the horse's face, this happens mainly with the jointed snaffle and not with the mullen.

TO FIT When the reins are attached to the floating rings more pressure is transferred to the nose. In a less severe form the nosepiece is attached to the front of an ordinary snaffle so that by tightening the nosepiece you can take away a lot of pressure from the mouth. Both types of nosepiece can be adjusted so that the pressure can be transferred from the mouth to the nose or a combination of both in differing degrees.

The Rockwell

This bridle uses the same type of nosepiece as the Citation but has only one bit. It can be a loose-ring jointed snaffle or even a snaffle with a medium-ported or mullen mouthpiece. The nosepiece has two rings that attach to the mouthpiece between the corner of the horse's lip and the cheek of the bit and is adjustable so that the rider can apply more or less nose pressure. As the rein is applied the bit is pulled back in the mouth and the action is on the corners of the lips and the nose if a jointed snaffle is used, and on the tongue, the bars of the mouth and the nose if a mullen mouth is used.

TO FIT The bit must be the right size for the mouth as the rings of the nosepiece sit right next to the corners of the lips: too narrow a bit would certainly cause rubbing. The nosepiece should sit as high as possible on the nose without pulling the bit up in the horse's mouth and is supported by a face strap.

Newmarket

Rockwell

71

Combination nose bridle and bit

This is often an American gag with a hackamore front attached which has the combined effect of a gag plus strong nose and poll pressure. The bridle must be of good quality because badly made versions tend to have the nosepiece far too long which allows the nosepiece to drop too far down the nose causing severe discomfort.

combination nose bridle and bit

TO FIT As with all bridles using downward nose pressure, the nosepiece must not be fitted too low and a careful check of all pressure points for possible bruising and rubbed places needs to be made constantly. The bit should fit neatly into the corners of the mouth following the principles of fitting a loose-ring snaffle. The nosepiece should sit comfortably on the face above the soft fleshy part of the nose not on the nostrils. Extra padding may be needed at the back of the noseband to prevent rubbing. You may find that you have to have shorter cheekpieces on the bridle to ensure the noseband fits at the level of a cavesson noseband.

The Scawbrigg

This simple form of bitless bridle is made of a padded nosepiece which is usually lined with chamois leather or sheepskin. The nosepiece is supported by a small piece of leather attached to the cheek of the bridle. The back is a wide padded piece resting on the horse's jawbones passing through the rings of the nosepiece to become reins. There should be a supporting strap fastening at the back passing through a loop on the chinpiece to stop the noseband twisting round.

TO FIT It should be fitted three or four fingers' width above the nostrils so that the action does not interfere with the horse's breathing. This bridle can also be used in conjunction with a bit. If a bit *is* used, it is most important that the bit headpiece is fitted in a way that ensures that the Scawbrigg nosepiece is the closest thing to the face. With the Scawbrigg reins on the

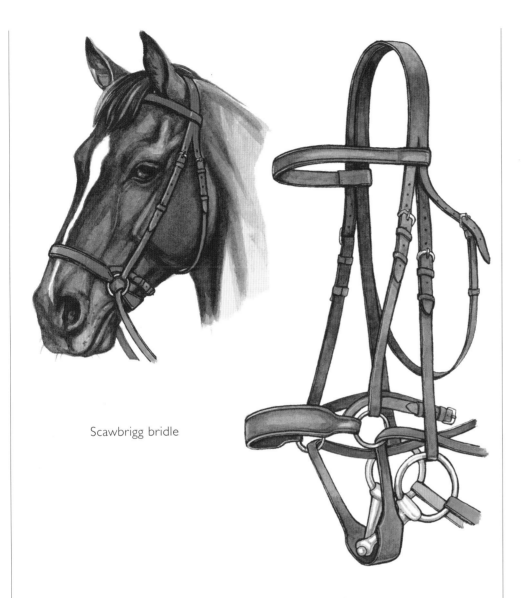

Scawbrigg bridle

nosepiece and a separate set of reins on the bit, you can carefully work the horse between bit pressure and nose pressure in varying degrees.

BR Equi bridle

This bitless bridle works on a sliding pulley system. When the reins are used, the two pulleys are drawn up the cheeks putting pressure simultaneously on the nose and on the poll; the pulleys are prevented from sliding too close to the eyes by clips attached to the nosepiece. It has a potentially very strong action and needs a lot of padding at the back of the nosepiece.

TO FIT Great care must be taken to fit the nosepiece high enough to ensure that it does not drop too low and interfere with the horse's breathing. The chain nosepiece consists of three chains: one at each side of the face and one in the curb groove. There must be a rubber curb guard, or some similar padding, between the chain in the curb groove and the horse's jaw to prevent the bridle being too severe. As with a curb chain, the chains must all be twisted flat so that they lie comfortably on the horse's face and in the curb groove.

BR Equi bridle

Side-pull hackamore

This is a Western bridle which comprises a headpiece, cheekpieces and a browband attached to a rope-fronted noseband or a leather-covered rope noseband. The reins attach to Ds sewn on to the noseband at the bottom of each cheekpiece. The idea of this form of bridle is that a young horse can be first long reined and then ridden from the nose. As the formative training of young horses begins with control on the nose they are already accustomed to this form of control. The horse can then be long reined again from the nose with the addition of a bit attached to the bridle. The bit is held in the mouth without any use being made of it. When a rider is added to the equation, the young horse is ridden first on the nose alone and then with an extra rein attached to the bit. Gradually, less nose pressure is used and more bit pressure so that the work flows through and is clearly understood by the horse.

TO FIT As with any head device that relies on nose pressure, the fit must not interfere with the horse's breathing so must be sufficiently high on the nose not to touch the fleshy nostrils but not high enough to rub the projecting cheekbones. The noseband should fit the nose snugly so that there is minimal side to side movement as the reins are used. There are also supporting straps to help keep the noseband at the correct level.

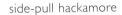
side-pull hackamore

19 IN-HAND RESTRAINT

W E ARE OFTEN AT OUR MOST vulnerable when leading our horses, especially if small and light in stature and leading a large horse, or if the horse is difficult to lead. It does not take a bright horse very long to realise that we cannot control them if they really put up a concerted effort to escape from us in a headcollar.

Simple tasks such as walking our horses to and from the field can become quite frightening. The following two pieces of equipment are specifically designed for in-hand work and do not require a bit, thus making it easier to remove the restraint from the horse's head without the added risk of him throwing his head up and getting the bit caught on his front teeth.

restrainer noseband

Restrainer noseband

This device is used to great effect on strong youngstock, stallions and difficult-to-lead animals. It has a padded sprung-steel nose-piece and crossover straps passing behind the face attached to an ordinary lead rein or rope and is used in conjunction with a headcollar.

As the lead rein is pulled, the cross straps tighten the sprung nosepiece and firm pressure is applied to the nose, as soon as the horse stops pulling and the handler regains control and relaxes the pull on the horse's head, the pressure on the nose is released.

TO FIT The restrainer noseband is fitted to a conventional headcollar using bit straps or sprung snaps. The headcollar is fitted high on the horse's face so that the restrainer is at the height of a drop noseband; if fitted lower it would interfere with the horse's breathing.

Be Nice halter

This halter is a restraint and training device to be used when leading and training your horse in close in-hand work. It works on the principle of instantly applied, firm poll and nose pressure; as the horse resists you pull down on the rope attached to the halter and the device tightens on the nose and the poll. As soon as the horse complies and the handler slackens the rope, the pressure is instantly released. It is made of nylon and dacron braid which is very soft, strong and pliable and which tightens and releases through the metal rings easily. Over the horse's poll area there are smooth, cast bronze bobbles that push down into the horse's head just behind the poll to reinforce the downward signal.

Be Nice halter

TO FIT There are four American sizes so it can be quite an art to pick the right size for your horse. The best way is to take a headcollar that fits your horse well, then, when you go to buy a Be Nice halter, you have a size guide.

20 LUNGEING AND DRIVING WHIPS

I T IS IMPORTANT TO GET THE RIGHT WHIP for the right job. If your lunge whip does not reach your horse when you wish to correct him, or the whip is too heavy for you to carry in the right position for the duration of the work, and if, when driving, your whip reaches the nose of your carriage horse, then you have the wrong whip.

Too short

If your whip is too short you cannot possibly correct your horse quickly and efficiently as each instant occurs. If you have to leap towards your horse to correct him you have to let the lunge line tension go thus allowing your horse to veer off and shoot forward and then he has to be steadied again. Or, if you have to reel the lunge line in, by the time you have done so, the horse has probably picked up speed because he realises the whip is getting closer. With the correct length of whip you simply swing the whip, tap your horse and proceed.

Too heavy

The balance of a whip is very important. If the whip you are using is so heavy that it is difficult to hold and balance, then your wrist will get very tired and you will not be able to hold or use the whip properly.

Too long

If the whip is too long, then not only is the balance difficult to manage but you are also going to be making corrections in the wrong place. If you are lungeing you could be hitting your horse on the opposite shoulder and driving him in towards you. If you are driving with too long a whip, you could be hitting your horse on the neck or in the face.

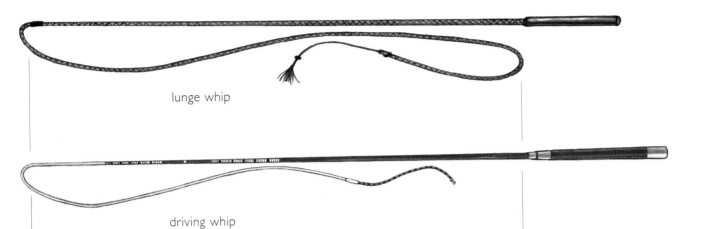

lunge whip

driving whip

Too bulky

If you have very small hands, a whip with a thick heavy stock (hand part) is going to be very difficult to hold comfortably for a period of time.

Retailers will not mind if you try out whips to find one that you are comfortable with, although I did once nearly hit two people at a trade show overzealously trying driving whips for balance. Retailers are usually only too happy to order for you if you require something different.

21 HORSE PROTECTION

FOR ALL FORMS OF SCHOOLING you need to think about protection and/or support for the horse's legs. It will depend on what type of work you intend to do and on the age, fitness and health of your horse as to which type of boot or bandage is going to be most suitable.

One of the most important things to remember if you are using boots or bandages is that not only must the horse's legs be scrupulously clean and free from veterinary products but so must any boot or bandage that is put on them. Any boot or bandage that is dirty will cause sores and rubs. The majority of brushing boots are made of some form of nylon or neoprene, both materials tend to make the surface they cover heat up and sweat. A lot of medicinal cooling and healing products specifically list in their information that they should either not be covered or that they should not be tightly bandaged. It is most important if you have a horse who is in work but who needs a supportive boot or bandage and also some sort of medicinal product applied that you apply the product correctly and stick to the recommended guidelines.

TO FIT You need to make sure all boots and bandages are put on correctly and are very secure so that they will never come undone and cause an accident. As a general rule you should be able to fit your index finger comfortably into the top of any boot or bandage. They should be the same tension all the way down the legs and any fastening should only be as tight as the boot or bandage itself, never tighter because this creates a tighter band that digs into the leg.

BOOTS

Brushing Boots

In order to be effective, brushing boots must meet certain standards otherwise it is really not worth putting them on the horse's legs. The base material must be thick enough to actually afford some protection. The inner pad that runs down the leg has to be a good shape to cover the inside of the leg, and to cup the fetlock joint. The hind boots should have a larger padded area over the fetlock joint as some horses brush the back lower half of the joint continually. The materials used must be pliable and mould to the shape of the leg. The boot should be long enough to cover the whole area from just under the knee to just below the fetlock. Lastly, it should have an easy but secure and effective fastening.

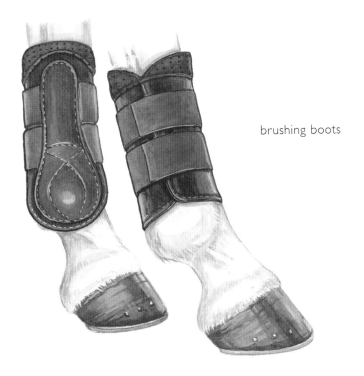

brushing boots

Tendon Boots

There are various tendon boot designs and you need to choose one which suits your purpose best. If you need a tendon boot to protect the tendons of a jumping horse then use an open-fronted boot which will leave the front

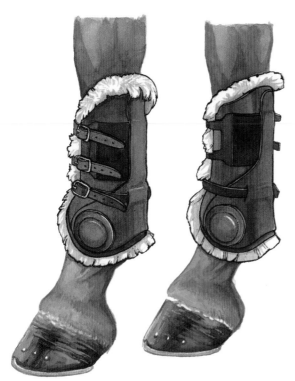

leather tendon boots

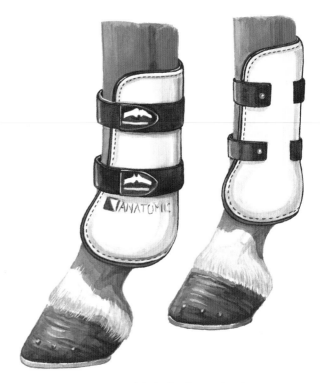

moulded plastic tendon boots

of the horse's leg exposed and keep his sensitivity to knocked poles while protecting the tendons from being struck by the hind feet. For polo a much more substantial boot is required to go over polo bandages to give protection from hind-foot strike, protection from other horses during riding off and the possibility of being hit by a mallet.

Speedy cut boots

A speedy cut injury often occurs when fast work is being carried out, it is usually a high cut either just under the knee or hock. This boot is a brushing boot that is made much longer and higher than a conventional brushing boot thus extending the area covered to protect the lower knee and hock. Again, they must be well made and mould to the leg staying firmly in place during any fast galloping or jumping.

Professional's Choice sports medicine boots

These boots were designed for the performance horse or pony; they give exceptional protection and support and should be used for specific

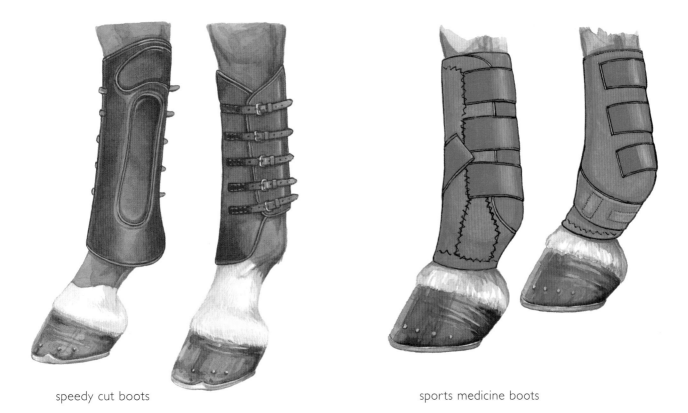

speedy cut boots   sports medicine boots

purposes. The boots warm the horse's legs creating a moist environment
that enhances blood circulation, and support and protect the legs from side
impact and concussion. They can be used for horses that are sound and
competing in rigorous conditions such as cross-country jumping or FEI
carriage marathons or for fast schooling work or prolonged trotting work
on the road. Most of our work with horses is preparation for competition
and not actually competing, it makes sense, therefore, to protect and
support the legs so that we can actually get to the event with a sound horse.
They are also very good boots to use for: a horse who has had an injury and
is being brought back into work, older horses with weaknesses and horses
prone to tearing around their paddocks with gay abandon thus running the
risk of the vet having to be called yet again.

It is important to get the sizing right and if you are looking for a high
degree of proven protection and support make sure you buy the correct
boot and not a lookalike. For horses with long hind cannon bones there
is a high-top version that is 2 in longer than the standard boot.

Skid boots

These are specifically designed to protect the ergot and the underneath of the hind fetlock joint and are mostly used for the training and working of Western horses and polo ponies. These horses in particular use sliding halts in their work, that is, as they halt or turn in a fast gait, the hind joints are under so much pressure that they are actually pushed into and slide on the floor. The boots are made of thick neoprene with a thickly covered inner brushing pad and an extra rubber pad covering the lower fetlock area cupping the back of the fetlock joint. New versions now bend under the horses ergot and extend at the back to wrap around the upper back pastern area so that no dirt can slide into the boots as a polo pony or a reining horse slides to a halt.

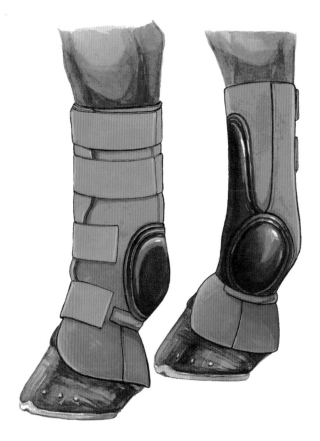

skid boots

Combination Boots

These incorporate a brushing boot and a bell boot in one boot. Some versions do not allow for enough freedom of movement but Professional's Choice have now designed a hinged version that does not inhibit any movement. This is the ultimate in all-round protection. You need to make sure that the boot is firmly secured to the leg so that it does not slip down as that will cause the bell boot to be pushed lower on the foot as well. The boot should be wrapped firmly onto the horse's leg but you should be able to get an index finger comfortably into the boot at the top.

Fetlock boots

Fetlock boots are designed to protect the fetlock area on the hind legs and are most commonly seen on jumping horses. They come in a variety of materials from neoprene to leather with neoprene or sheepskin removable inner pieces. They are designed for inner fetlock joint protection only and if your horse is prone to brushing elsewhere on the hind limbs, you really need to have a full brushing boot instead.

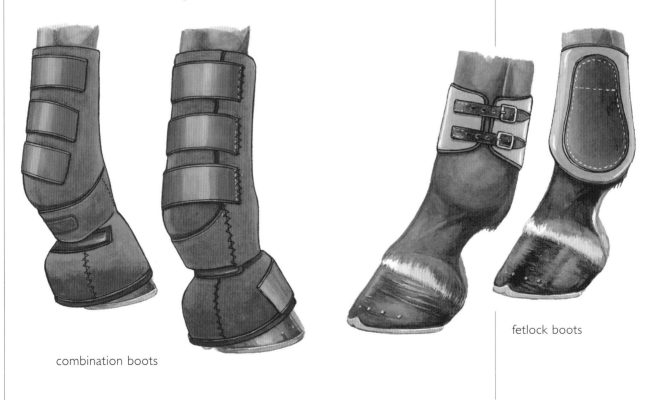

combination boots

fetlock boots

Overreach boots

Also called bell boots, these boots are specifically designed to protect the coronary band and the bulbs of the heels. They are usually worn only on the front legs but can be worn all round in, for instance, the marathon section of carriage driving trials as extra protection is often needed, particularly when more than one horse is being driven. The ordinary overreach boots, either the pull-on version or the tab or Velcro fastening types, all give very good protection against overreach wounds caused by the horse striking himself but the padded bell boot also gives a high degree of protection against treads received from the close proximity of other horses, as in the game of polo for instance.

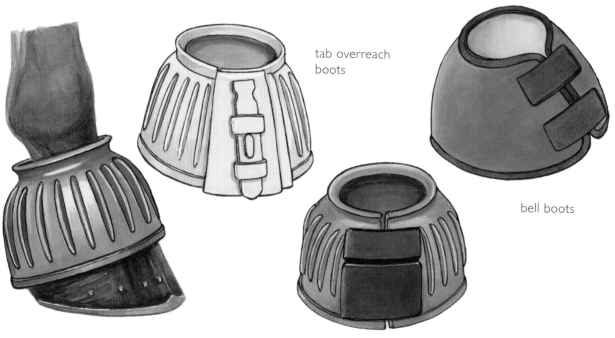

tab overreach
boots

bell boots

rubber overreach boots

Velcro overreach boots

Sausage boots

These boots are a piece of dense rubber tubing with a leather strap running through the middle which is fastened around the horse's back pastern on one hind leg only. They are used for a horse that continually brushes in one place, just marking the coronary band on one hind leg, for example, each time he is worked.

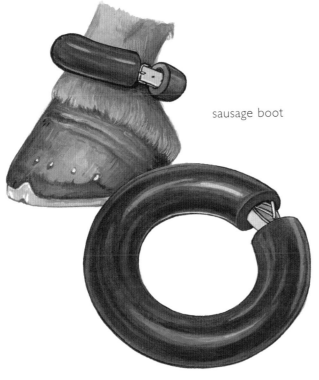

sausage boot

BANDAGES

Elastic exercise bandages

These come in 3in or 4in widths and in a large variety of colours. Exercise bandages should be put on very evenly and firmly and always over Gamgee or Fybagee. The securing tapes should be flat and only as tight as the bandage, no tighter, the fastening should be on the outside of the leg and, to ensure they remain safely fastened, either sewn or bandage-taped into place.

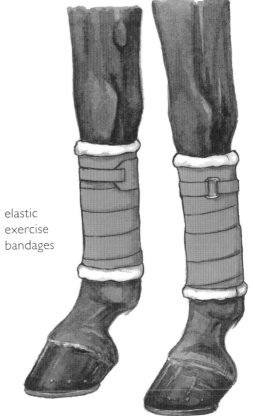

elastic exercise bandages

Polo bandages

Polo bandages are available in a wide variety of colours and are designed to be bandaged directly onto the horse's leg. They are made of soft stretchy Polatec and mould to the shape of the leg as you bandage. They can be used to just cover the cannon bone and upper fetlock area or be bandaged lower to cover the fetlock joint as well. They are very useful for supportive protection for youngsters with extravagant action as you can bandage down to the pastern and then meet the bottom of the bandage with over-reach boots. Polo ponies will need additional protection in the form of skid boots over the bandages on the hind legs, tendon or heavy brushing boots on the front legs plus bell boots on the front hooves to prevent the heels being trodden on.

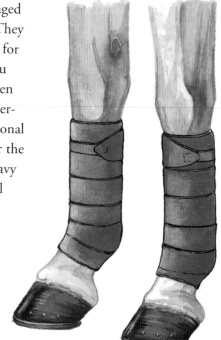

polo bandages

22 RIDER PROTECTION

I T DOES NOT MATTER HOW EXPERIENCED or inexperienced you are, anyone can have an accident, even the most well-schooled horse can have an off day or be startled through no fault of his own. A whole season's competing, or even your life, can be put in jeopardy when all you needed to do was put on a riding hat, a body protector, a pair of gloves or a more sensible pair of boots!

Hats

You can have an accident at any time anywhere around your horse. It would be unreasonable to expect you to wear a hat whenever you go near your horse but you have to be sensible and it is only good horsemanship to wear your hat when riding, lungeing and long reining your horse. It would also be sensible to wear a hat when leading a horse known to be difficult to the field or when leading and handling young horses. Make sure that the hat you own is the correct British Safety Standard, that you have it correctly fitted and if you have had an accident involving a blow to your hat, get a new one. Modern hats are more bulky and no longer look as neat and dashing as they used to but they are far safer than the old standards. The reason for the bulk is the depth of padding required to make the hat safe.

TO FIT The idea is for the hat to fit the whole surface area of the skull as well as possible. The modern hat is bulky and very solid and needs to be fitted by someone trained to fit them. As the hat is placed on the head it should go on with just a little resistance but not so that it pushes in on the brow or the back of the head. It must be deep enough to come to rest just above the ears and approximately ½in above the eyebrows. Among the makes of hats the depths vary so it may be necessary to try one or two different types to establish if your head is shallow or deep from the top of the ear to the crown of the head. Children's heads can be the most difficult to fit as children often have a domed forehead and the back of the head slopes dramatically into the neck. In this case you can often get your fingers up into the inside of the hat at the back. It is easier if the hat is always placed on the head from front to back and a little hat packing is placed at the back of the helmet to take up some of the space. The hat is not safe and is not designed to be worn on the back of the head or without the strapping, or harness, done up. It should be worn squarely on the brow with the strapping firmly in place.

Body Protectors

There are several body protectors on the market now which are very well designed and have a high degree of comfort and safety. It is vitally important that you go to a good saddlery shop and get informed advice and, more importantly, the correct fitting for your size and shape. What you have to remember is that it is actually body armour and must give a good degree of protection, so it is going to feel a little restrictive until you are accustomed to wearing it.

TO FIT Again, you are looking for a protector that fits your body shape as well as possible without restricting movement or the ability to take up the jumping position or to simply get on your horse! It is very important that the body protector is the correct length. How many times do you see children with the top of the armour inches above their shoulders and the head peeping out from the neck? This is due to very poor fitting and advice at point of sale. The front of the armour must lie approximately 1 in above the protruding hip bones, so that the rider can comfortably assume the jumping position any amount of times and come upright again without the armour rising up. If the armour is too long, each time the rider flexes at the waist the armour gets pushed up and, as it is fitted tightly to the torso, it cannot then settle back down into place. The back of the armour should cover as much of the spine as possible without hitting the cantle of the saddle. The armholes should be cut away at the front to allow freedom while still protecting the collarbone.

Gloves

Using gloves when riding, driving, lungeing or long reining your horse should be an essential part of a rider's or whip's (carriage driver's) equipment. They not only protect hands from accidents they actually maintain a far better contact on the rein and afford real protection when leading horses with a rope. As with all clothing you do tend to get what you pay for and a good quality pair of leather gloves not only looks smart but also lasts longer. It is always a good idea to keep expensive gloves for working your horse or competing and a series of less expensive pairs for stable work.

TO FIT The fit of a pair of gloves is very much a personal matter but it is important that you do not restrict the circulation of the fingers, especially in winter, nothing is worse than fingers you cannot feel. Do make sure you know the rules of correct attire for your chosen discipline so that you wear the correct colour and type.

Footwear

I had to have my foot stitched in the early hours of the morning some years ago and the nurse asked if I always brought horses in from the field in gold strapped sandals and an evening gown! The answer should have been that I knew the dangers and was too experienced to do such a thing!

Correct footwear with the right degree of protection is always easier to wear in the winter but, even though it gets hot in the summer, you should always wear footwear designed for the activity: protection from being trodden on, support should you need to run, a decent heel for riding and a safe fastening that will not catch on anything.

TO FIT Children's feet in particular need careful consideration. Very small slim children are much safer in jodhpur boots than in rubber boots. The jodhpur boot fits the foot well and is firmly held in place by strong elastic at the ankle. The long rubber boot is often too long for the small child, gaps at the top mean the boots can catch on parts of the saddle as exercises are done and the boots are likely to fall off when riding without stirrups is practised.

USEFUL ADDRESSES

Gloster and Restrainer Nosebands
Spalding Saddlery,
Cliffords Farm, Ovington, Richmond, North Yorkshire DL11 7DD
Tel: 01833 627210   Fax: 01833 627562

BR Schooling Equipment
Bieman de Haas BV,
PO Box 8, 6658 ZG Beneden-Leeuwen, Netherlands
Tel: (+ 31) 0487 597880   Fax: (+31) 0487 591070

Harbridge Training Aid and Worcester Noseband
Shires Equestrian Products,
15 Southern Avenue, Leominster, Herefordshire HR6 0QF
Tel: 01568 613600   Fax: 01568 613599

Pessoa Training System
R.W.A., 9 Station Road, Morcott, Oakham, Rutland LE15 9DX
Tel: 01572 747595   Fax: 01572 747686

Side Pull Bridles and Be Nice Halters
The Western Department,
Rookery Farm Equestrian, Shabbington, Aylesbury, Buckinghamshire HP18 9HF
Tel and Fax: 01844 201656

Wels Cavesson
Turf and Travel,
The Old Bakery, Wexham Street, Wexham, Buckinghamshire SL3 6NX
Tel: 01753 730099   Fax: 01753 790099

General Enquires
Tally Ho Farm, Crouch Lane, Winkfield, Berkshire SL4 4RZ
Tel: 01344 885373   Fax: 01344 891482

INDEX